John McKeown

Sea of Leaves

First published in 2009
by Waterloo Press (Hove)
95 Wick hall
Furze Hill
Hove BN3 1NG

Printed in Palatino 11pt by
One Digital
54 Hollingdean Road
East Sussex BN2 4AA

© John McKeown 2009
All rights remain with the author.

Cover design and Typesetting © Matilda Persson 2009

John McKeown is hereby identified as author of this work in accordance with Section 77 of the Copyright, Designs and Patents Act 1988

This book is sold subject to the condition that it shall not, by way of trade or otherwise, be lent, resold, hired out or otherwise circulated without the author's prior consent in any form of binding or cover other than that in which it is published and without a similar condition including this condition being imposed on the subsequent purchaser.

A CIP record for this book is available
from the British Library

ISBN 978-1-906742-08-9

By the same author

Looking Toward Inis Oírr (South Tipperary Arts, 2004)
Samhain (Waterloo Press, 2004)
Amour Improper (Hub Editions, 2005)

Acknowledgements

Thanks to the editors of the following journals in which some of these poems have previously appeared: *Cyphers, Southword, The Shop, Dream Catcher, Aireings, Borderlines* (Anglo-Welsh Poetry Society), *Other Poetry* and *The Recusant* website.

Contents

Samhain	15
On the Fifth Floor	16
Passing in the Office Corridor	17
Rush Hour	18
Suburbia	19
White Dwarf	20
Smog	21
Joy	22
The Building Opposite	23
Apollo House	24
Plague	25
Hippocampus	26
That Kiss	27
Wish	28
Gondolas	29
White Cats	30
Embedded	31
The Hundred Years Sex War	32
Unkindled	33
Earthly Treasure	34
Against Nature	35
Foxes	36
Taboo	37
The Old Religion	38
Arguments in Pompeii	39
Waitress in Cafe Imperial, Prague	40
Haircut	41
Sacrament	42
Fitou	43
Brandy & Soda	44
Eclipse	45
Masque	46
Tokaji	47
Scott's Bar	48
The Spirit of Dublin	49
Fellow Men	50
The Flightless Bohemian	51

Transit	52
The Fishermen	53
Ornithology	54
Gulled	55
Sails	56
Sea-Flight	57
Llandudno	58
Gronant	59
The Suir at Clonmel	60
Cormorant	61
Genius Loci	62
Olympian	63
One Moment	64
Purpose	65
The Tinned Food Eaters	66
View From The Station	67
Twilight	68
Twilight Moon	69
Venus at Seapoint	70
At Home	71
Lost Chances	72
Anxious Animal	73
Will	74
A Dublin Bell	75
Letting Go	76
Tree Trimming	77
Roadside Trees	78
Chestnut Trees	79
The Craft	80
Radiant	81
Ferris Wheel	82
All Over	83
Galway Bay	84
Canary	85
Diplomacy	86
Snail's Pace	87
Burning Peat Briquettes	88
Ship at Dusk	89
Wexford Harbour	90

'Poetry is what happens when nothing else can.'
Charles Bukowski

'What makes the bitter so sweet? – Hunger.'
Alcuin of York, 8th Century

Sea of Leaves

Samhain

Body of life tap at my door
tap at my darkened door tonight,
slip in and draw me to my height
let my hot seed break and enter.

Unspent, gather me once more,
tear my burden in your breast,
body of life tap at my door
tap at my darkened door tonight.

I'll scatter ashes on the floor
to take our strange escape's imprint,
ashes of the death I wore,
the living death, the suit of wood.

Body of life tap at my door.

On the Fifth Floor

Brown carpet and nondescript
beige walls, the red eyes
of weighted, freshly-varnished doors
waiting to be swiped green.

A state-of-the-art canteen,
seating as on a channel ferry,
somewhere comfortable
to struggle over the crossword.

No clue needed as to what's off
the stripped silence of the corridor,
each of those boxes a variant of Hell,
Sheol, Inferno, Underworld.

And in-between, like bad breath,
the smell of Purgatory,
of rotten mind, dead spirit.
No poetic fantasy, this is real,

I've seen Virgil and Dante, suited,
whispering through the fire doors.

Passing in the Office Corridor

Our mouths pop,
slowly,
like goldfish,
though there's nothing
gold about us.
Its grey
recognizing brown,
minnow
hailing stickleback.

Glassy-eyed,
we mouth in tandem
the bare, airless minimum
accident forces from us.
An ambiguous Aloha
part politesse,
part loathing.

The latter at least I
like to think.
Faintly colouring my bit
of this shared element
this gutless void we inhabit.

Rush Hour

Bright and pure
the almost full
circle of the Moon.

Elysium,
mute with wonder
at the cold rush hour,

at Styx, Acheron,
Phlegethon, Lethe,
and Cocytus,
river of wailing.

Suburbia

Suburbia almost makes sense,
dripping with stillness, peace
under the rain-washed, wild, calamitous sky.

Seeming to reflect a deeper order,
a natural stability, my restless, unmortgageable
over-heated temperament's too thick to realize.

This is the heart of things, the good life:
a house set well back, two cars in the drive,
garden trim or self-consciously unkempt.

Then two semi-detachees conversing as I pass,
his golf's improved with those new clubs...
Suburbia's a graveyard, and these are it's living dead.

White Dwarf

Among the rush hour crowd
every one a star
I am a white dwarf.

More compact than those
so compact
that one teaspoonful
of my carbonized core
would break the city's throat.

Fold on material fold
I'm still collapsing

a spirit worming out of flesh.

Smog

Like a gangrenous wound,
mass banality's signature,
the smog seeping into the sky.
Perversely comforting too,
this smutty sign of mankind's presence
against the mute vastness.
Like the smoke-stained ceiling of a pub,
yellow-coated witness
to the good, the bad, the beautiful,
witness to life under the wheels of time.

But no ham-fisted romanticising of it.
That layer of filth is one city's
pus-filled ecological bootprint.
The other boot's on the accelerator.

Joy

Like spots
of a sun-shower in Hell
my baby daughter's
eyes and smiles

as we push her through
the city streets
where every joy
has died.

The Building Opposite

A browning tome
in which lives are pressed
under the screw of work
and not a trickle of juice flows out.

Through tomb-shaped windows
the shaded signs of life
are broken and broken again
into a fine white powder.

An ashen mizzle of dreams
I can feel from here
as through the crack in my head I twitch
my unreconstructed antennae.

Apollo House

Something accusatory
in the bronze flood
of the setting Sun.

As if it would have temples
where offices are,
worshippers, not drudges.

As if it were no
mere play of light;
and we were gods, not corpses.

Plague

They're not the bees' knees
these women

though their tits are thick
with pollen

and beds of roses sleep
in each eye.

Think more along the lines
of locusts

their clicking joints a plague
on peace of mind

the leaving of you arid
unsatisfied.

Shut the senses up
when they knock

when they darken the Sun
with their wings

be a shrinking violet
deadly nightshade

a Venus fly-trap green
on your own bitter sap.

Hippocampus

Far too elegant
but I choose it
for my mascot:
the Sea-Horse.

I love its disempowered
proud, equine look,
as if it were riding out
to the last flicker of current,
a Sea-God's wrath.

A Sea-God's sick humour too,
this stallion under the waves' spell,
its limbs bound
into one pre-
hensile forelock.

Apparently cursed,
but it kicks back
with its pregnant reversal
of the order of nature.
And latterly, reminds me

there are things
in this world
more mouth-watering
than women.

That Kiss

As inexplicable as the kiss
the remembrance.
The sudden gift of her lips
in the teeth of everything.

Memory and kiss both
equally unsolicited.
Mouths, hands, tongues,
hotly intertwined

taking the moment by surprise.

Wish

I wish I were the sea
unfolding wave
by wave in you.

I wish I were shell
and stone feeling your
deep encroachment.

I wish I were the tide
drawn to your swell
and we woke entangled

inseparable in the windrow.

Gondolas

Gondolas empty as coffins
knocking on green canal water,
redolent of wood in winter,
the tethered hollows of your absence.

At the full the sinking Sun's rays
through whose light we'll never steer,
gondolas empty as coffins
knocking on green canal water.

The Basilica, Lido, islands,
all blent in one golden vapour,
and the scattered cafe tables
bare in the air of the dying year.

Gondolas empty as coffins.

White Cats

Three white cats
with shy hostility
in their eyes
befur our steps.
Like parts of a broken
white body trying
to fit itself back together.
As we try to fit.
The cradle
of our hands
never knitting
breaking again
as we step
through them.

Embedded

I can almost smell
the Sun on the tree
in the road where I lived
telling me how simple it was.

I could leave her
and however stricken
life would renew itself.
But I couldn't make

that simple break.
My vigourous roots
were busy drinking
at pain's water table.

The Hundred Years Sex War

No more than a skull
scrotum-skinned,
wisps of white hair.
But she drags him over
each and every coal,
still hot, and he submits
to the reins.

She pauses to dab
crocodile tears
in a compact.
He looks on Hell,
draws her close,
thinking to embrace
all of it.

Unkindled

To be rolled in a touch
like a log held in fire
caught top to toe in a sheath
of hot breath
the skin of my everyday impurities
burning
a long lean canoe of soul coalescing.

O your tongue would coat
every fleck and knot of me
and receiving you, filled
to the rounded roots with you,
I would be seaworthy.

We would pitch and toss, awhile,
then glide gently,
into the burned-down dark,
your weight laid in mine.

Earthly Treasure

Into the grave with you
and that bright hour
I didn't see was trimmed with love.

Into the grave that hotel
and the pines laced with ice,
and the river, and the guests.

Into the grave that world of earth,
the February sun of that day,
and all of that young you.

You were beautiful, I was blind,
but you are, will be, all
my shining grave goods.

Against Nature

I was liquefying in a pool of sweat
trying to penetrate my kindred spirit
before she flew east, forever.

Her trembles were like ripples of the sea
ready to enclose me, but I died
each time I nosed into them.

I kept on, blind as something hatched
high and dry, trying to reach the Ocean.
Until it dawned, and the light set

like stone. Hard enough for the birds
to walk on.

Foxes

She's outfoxed me
with forgiveness,
run me to my own
amoral earth,
where I must dig deep
to find the finest,
wireiest, sophistical roots,
to secure forbidden pleasure.

Far too wise
to lick her paws
on the moral high ground,
she sheds her love like snow,
til everything is out of shape
and shining,
and my least, lightest,
panting track

can be seen
across the distance.

Taboo

I was the apple
she was the ground,
she rose once
but I didn't fall.
I was fixed by fear
to a taboo tree,
while she was one
unbridled whisper
that snaked
from offered lips
like Summer flame.

That wish that shone
in her eyes out
of the darkness
of our shared blood,
is now the worm, regret,
keeping me slightly
rotten to the core.

The Old Religion

I thought it was her
but it was a wicker woman
I'd constructed,
rolled it up to a great height,
and set it burning
with my heart
screaming inside.

She can sense the smoke
and see my red eyes
when I get close,
but she's no goddess,
she cannot make them
clear blue,
she cannot make me
fruitful.

Arguments in Pompeii

This is all ancient history.
Here's where I stood
my back to the wall
a burnt shadow gesticulating.
Here's where she dealt
blow after gladiatorial blow,
a shade outlined in broken plaster.

And here's where we made up
time and time again,
this smudge, our bed,
below the cover of ash and lava.

Waitress in Cafe Imperial, Prague

Her hair a seam of gold,
she persists, spreading silently
under the killing weight
of compressed circumstance.

She arranges tables, brings beer,
smiles into massed
ignorant faces, while her fingers,
ministers of her soul's elegance

conduct concertos of beauty
unknown to her.

Haircut

It has all the makings
of a kiss,
her white fingers
with the scissors
pressing my cheek
near the mouth.
My heart briefly
rises to the spot
then sinks beneath the sheet
under the fine hair
pattering above.
How shaped she is to me,
her pale arms bent
like the beautiful
handles of a jug.
Her touch is light as breath,
and I obey.
And it is better than love.

Sacrament

In the name of unrequited lust
I invest this red seedless grape
with the flavour of your tongue.

I test your breast's warm full shape,
lift the amphora of your hips,
gently round the contour of your cape.

I reverence you in the chalice
of my mouth; break the soft skin, you
turn the grape to sweetness.

Fitou

The night she brought
the Fitou
I waited under the tree
hating, loving her.
In the flat I waited
in the sagging armchair
for her to call me
to the couch
and when she did
I came.
Obedient as sap
blind as blossom.

Brandy & Soda

A waning crescent
of brandy in my glass
while I grow dark with life.

Such quiet verdancy
such hush held
in horns of light!

All soon becomes
discordant, harsh,
a scrape of voices, plates.

Though I can leave,
having tasted, dissolved
in wafers of amber

a moment's completeness.

Eclipse

Corwen Churchyard, Wales, August 11th 1999

From the high street the cars fall quiet,
voices tensely admire what science is proving.
Here, I note how flowers seem more erect;
a cock, sensing betrayal, starts crowing.
A hush, like the hush off dew-soaked gardens
deepens, til the world's a web about to break:
the dead might writhe like shoots from out their graves,
or the Preaching Cross at which I sit, speak.
Some judgement, condemnation, absolution,
gathered in the precipitant air, fine as a blade,
some logos of reconciliation.
No word comes but the chill, the deepening shade.
And this is not permitted long. Already
the Sun defies this moment's gravity.

Masque

Masques of air
subtly stirring
across my face.
The silent pomp
of passing time,
crowns offered
and withdrawn.
The very feel
of the shadowy
marching play,
the brush of its
vaporous pageantry,
its exquisite
insubstantiality.
To float, lulled
by strokes of air,
the masks untied.
Feathery as water
fanned by a breeze
to deeper stillness.

Tokaji

Is it such a mistake
to try and live on
the smokey, dirty architecture?

Or the way the river gulls
at night
ride the waves of the Danube?

The autumn breeze
in the Buda streets
has an unspeakable, loaded subtlety.

And there is sweet, sweet Tokaji.

Scott's Bar

Intimations
of splendour
in the lamps
burning
hourlessly.
The rumbling
of the air-conditioner
like the funnel
of a liner.
And the waitress
at the edge
of the long bar
folding red napkins
round cutlery.
As I try
to flesh out
another
useless moment.

The Spirit of Dublin

A local drunk,
a twitchy, aged,
little deflated old ball,
muttering to himself.
But he drank that Guinness
so reverential,
like he was kissing
some ancient beloved.
For those seconds
he was fluid, inspiring as music.
Then half-way down
the landlord comes,
tone-deaf to all the shades
of the heart,
takes his pint,
gives him his coins back,
and throws him out.

Fellow Men

The station's cold
and we all move
through each other.
On the train we sit
as far apart
as possible
as though each
were a bad smell.
We rattle on
through station after station
city after city
country after country.
We rattle on
through the tunnel
of each others' eyes.

The Flightless Bohemian

Šenk Vbrovec Prague 1

The golden bees
have broke
the light flown.

The blind bodies
come and go
but all is dark
at the centre.

There's only me
watching for a glint
from the rushing pavement.

The gold pollen
on my fading fur.

Transit

It's almost endearing
the glee of astronomers
in the transit of Venus.

Kids with calculators and telescopes,
seeing not the largesse of the paternal Sun,
but beads on an abacus.

On the chimney opposite
I spy a gull-chick wobbling, fuzzy
against the white breast of its parent.

And watch entranced this fruitfulness
growing to the drop,
this seed of life in transit.

More moving than any
mechanic conjunction of planets.

The Fishermen

They stand against the light,
pillocks of Hercules in baggy jeans,
plying their rods over the water.

I could understand if I tried.
The stoic dalliance with chance,
the thrill of hooking unseen nature,

but I don't want to. Though their ease
among the smell of worms, maggots,
might be construed as truly philosophical,

fuck them.

Ornithology

Perched on a pinnacle of brick
in a nest of green weed,
only the gull's pearl-white breast makes sense.

A white lily of the sky neither
toiling or spinning,
sitting in God's eye amid the human rush.

A little feather-folded boat, an Ark
on an urban Ararat,
plump and bright with nature's purpose.

And bright with her own species of joy too,
this once-born phoenix,
to me, a mired ashen office statistic.

Gulled

Gulls in the grey brightness.
The same gulls crying
out of the green dark past.

With feathered ogham script
with sonic snowing chalk-dust
they mark the air I struggle in.

Careless if I hear or no
wheeling crying they go
scrawling down pillars of air

aural old runes of desire.

Sails

I catch sight of two white sails
like flames on the still sea.

Like birdwings, stiff, swiftly
moving apart, as if the hand of fate

were carving, allowing me to read.
Or were loosening a knot, widening

the moment's meridian
into a path I must take.

Or were merely tightening,
what is, what must be.

Sea-Flight

Like the beat of wings
the fall of the waves.

Flight upon infinite flight
of foam-white birds:

the Sea in mass migration.
Dying on an arc of sand.

Llandudno

Watching the waves unfold, unfurl
gentle, soft, in Llandudno Bay,
the essences of former days
subtle, roseate, powerful.

On air as murmurs in a shell
the voices of old unspent joy,
watching the waves unfold, unfurl,
gentle, soft, in Llandudno Bay.

Beloved ones shift behind the veil
thinning in the Sun's last rays,
their beauty bliss about to fall,
a kiss as quick, as salt, as spray,

watching the waves unfold, unfurl.

Gronant

Gronant North Wales, 1967-70

We ran rings round the Sun, barefoot,
til it stood, enchanted by our energy.
In our favourite circle of sand dunes, thoughtless,
we forged our childhood's paradise.

The beach, vast, clean, pure as a new prayer-book,
its unprintable text in snakes of stinging sand.
The sea in the wind, one vast breath never caught,
or the flame of the blue-sky snuffed.

And guilty desire for the pink-bikinied girl,
spying on her through parted swords of dune-grass.
Feeling her breath in the caravanned dark, as I ached
for the clasp of her slim arms and legs.

How the small hills towered behind the village,
how the road steepened into the sky.
And the pub up there that we filled out,
a charming, tone-deaf, von Trapp Family.

I shudder to think of Gronant now,
tacky concrete, shopping centre, beach litter-strewn.
There was a ramshackle, weather-beaten store
where postcards curled, where wind-chimes blew,

I can almost recall its indefinable odour…
And the sunsets, the trickle of the streams,
glass-thin, ribbed with fish, cool on our feet.
Those suns never quite set; we never quite went home.

The Suir at Clonmel

Swift, the river's breathing,
deep the draught of asphodel
from watery head to root
in the river grass' waving.

The honey meadows race,
cold, unseen, unsweet,
trumpeted richness soundless
through the hives of industry.

Sharp as loss a leaf blows
in the pirouetting water's wind,
essences of autumns gone
through those sunless folds.

And vaguest wishes go with it,
amorphous desires follow,
red as the heart's unthreaded sack,
darkening the current.

Cormorant

The cormorant does
what Jesus did
without the publicity.

It stands securely
in the waves
on an invisible rock.

Not even remotely
proferring the keys
to any kingdom.

Genius Loci

There are places
where God's body
pokes through
the coat of the world.

He doesn't care
who sees the suggestive whiteness
of his skin, or how
maddening it might be.

Even God gets bored
with the world he must wear, wants
to stretch
in his nakedness.

When I turn the corner
and see his loins' beauty
piled in whitenesses of cloud
above the sea

I make a point of giving him
every encouragement.

Olympian

Summers of long ago
in the lit leaves.
Bright, timeless days
when we fought and played
blithe as young gods.

Skies of North Wales
in branches' blue tracery,
the Great Orme, Gronant, Rhyll,
we raced in the inexhaustible.
It fuels me still,

these hobbled, immortal longings.

One Moment

For one moment
even the smog is beautiful.
The blue cupola of the sky
is a promise somehow kept.
And even I laugh,
looking down on my incredible mess
from a great height.

For one thought flutters down
like a lone white feather.
At this moment
God is like me:
pure irresponsibility.

Purpose

I live for the moment
the sweet dirty foul moment
that opens in the dust of the world
and stares it out for seconds.

I live for the moment
the moment that flowers in me
the single bud its purity
distilled from impurity.

I live for the moment
like God who stocks all his being
in the nectar of a flower
that blooms wildly as it fades.

The Tinned Food Eaters

We were in the mouth of a cave
drying, eating something out of a tin
as the rain fell.

There were jokes, chat, consulting of maps,
soon we were gone — the wrong way.
Away from that sheltered entrance

that led into the deeps
where Proserpine's lotuses grew.

View From The Station

To be in that
pellucid twilight
stillness

washing out
from underneath
the scrawl
of the city.

To be fading
vast in that
momentary blend
of sea and air

forever
out of
the ordinary.

Twilight

Fine as the flit of a swallow,
the flutter of the white moth,
the pale half Moon's veiled face:
the gathering of twilight.

The flash of lighthouse and buoy
on the far cusp of the bay,
on the silvered paths of the sea,
and the stars not quite yet.
But coalescing; pearls of moistened breath
on the sky's deepening blue stained glass.

Untravelled but ancient, the light blooms
from an uncurtained window,
the thick head of a luminous flower
slowing the step, humming with the movement

of how all life happened long ago.

Twilight Moon

A shining rounded knee,
a luxurious glinting shoulder,
then her full forehead
emerges from the water.

Luna in her long bath
of straying evening cloud,
the goddess in the twilit lake,
washing out the sight of the world.

Though it gathers again, inevitably,
watching her white body dip and turn,
restores the true perspective,
that nothing can smear or stain.

Venus at Seapoint

A beautiful vase broken
and strewn across
the rubbish-littered sand.

Here and there a gleam
of the shattered
curved proportions.

And on the promise-bearing breeze
the tang
of sense-fulfilling perfection.
But where is She emergent?

Walking the warm waves
of the low tide far out
the fold of a world away.

At Home

Air is my home
clouds my furniture
that never goes
out of fashion.

No car, no breath
of petrol for me,
no mortgage, no kids
minted from money.

Just the round Earth
my bread and milk,
one with which
I am a giant.

Lost Chances

Looking back, the air
was thick with masts,
like a winter wood
at twilight.

Boats of every shape,
size, capacity, were there,
but I never stepped
on one of them.

The meanest of them
might've carried me
into that burning horizon
I watch slipping away.

Now all the masts are down
in the breaker's yard.
A few tubs on blocks.
And the stars are pitiless.

Anxious Animal

24 hours in a lather
over bills and money

bored and anxious
at life unquenched
slipping away.

While below the outside step
the mating frogs
still squat bold as brass

and silent
as deep pond water.

Will

Bind me in fragrant linen
seal me in a tomb-ship,
wake me when we dock
at the wharf of the next world.

I see its sun, its sky already,
I see how its waters move,
hands moulding flesh from stone,
I see its sharp sickle Moon.

Start the preparations now,
strop the blades, crack the jars,
mix unguents and herbs,
open my flesh like a sail.

A Dublin Bell

Out of the dry throat of Monday it rings
instilling the piquancy of escape.
In some Renaissance square, in porticoed shade,
with a dusty wine on which the Sun glints,
I've gone from grinding dullness to airy ripeness,
with life open to assume any shape,
and all time ahead, gently clustered, ripe,
as distant bells peel, lazy, ceremonious.

Stilled as a moth in some cathedral arch
shifting on its wings a folded icon,
I sit, the usher of rare feeling, thought,
from stir of noon to twilight's muslin hush.
One with the slow rung moment, unbroken,
as low stars, in faint sirocco breath are lit.

Letting Go

Autumn leaves
so crisply, gaily,
losing their touch.

I admire them,
peeling sharply
from the grey sky.

Rustling, croaking,
like tinsel songbirds
their parched old tune.

So dexterously
letting all the green
go to blazes.

Tree Trimming

They've sawn off the arms
that supported a headful of blossom,
they've cut the ground out
from under Spring and Summer,
now the seasons
have nowhere to roost.

They've left the trunk standing
with smooth-planed stumps of fresh wood,
like some warped cross
on which nothing's allowed
time to die or to live.
They've left a monument,

to the holocaust
of ignorance and stupidity.

Roadside Trees

Immeasurably tender the green shoots
out of the exhaust-blackened trees.
No bigger than snow-flakes some of them,
caught on the branch-tips, each unfolding
through a unique feat of balance.

Green stars that wont set but spread
til the sky is all gently rustling light.
Against the flaking bark they shine, flames
that tell earth's own old slow good time,
for me to set my darkness by.

Chestnut Trees

I want things hard as flint
but here are a mass
of chestnut leaves
dancing against the light.

I want Promethean bolts
to free me from the rock of self,
but in this orphic sway,
there seems no self, no chain.

Only limitless sensation
still to be pursued.
See the loose limbs of dryads there
fluttering at the open gates.

The Craft

No jeweller could mount
gems like this.
The rain droplets
on hair-fine birch tips.

And what alloy is it
makes them cling
so tenacious?
Til they seem more
like buds,
diamond-clear fruit,
efflorescence
of some unknown season?

There is no alloy,
no reason for this
gravity of beauty
that defies all human skill.

Just fingers of rain,
touching, tying,
slow and swift,
made this unprofitable orchard.

Radiant

The Moon radiant
at the vanquished heart
of silence.

Pouring all that's missing
through the bare branches,
transforming the rooves
into reflective platforms.

And the streets are silent
and the roads go nowhere,
for everything falls
into this still, one lit place.

Ferris Wheel

Like the Moon
grappled down
and taken apart
spar by spar
the riders scattered
like rays.

A monument
to the moment
packed up
and driven away
the levity over.

Just the tides
of sea and sky left
returning
to themselves.

All Over

A honeycomb
dark as a womb
once it was all ahead.

Now all is sacked
driven through by time
a rib-cage against light.

I need a new sum
added up outside
the mere calculation of years.

Dark capital incalculable
I can never touch
greening each bare moment.

Galway Bay

The moment folded up
before its quite unfolded,
discarded like a stone.

We are in the river
with watery hands
that cannot lace or hold,
memories only darker waters,
so everything must go.

The sky become a nitrous lick,
the hills crumbling into sea,
salt in everything equally
and a vast equanimity.

Canary

Its all a trap within a trap
we are twisted songbirds
here to amuse the gods.

So let them laugh,
I hope they choke
on their mortal delicacies and wine
as I go on, hopping
from perch to perch
tugging freedom from a song.

'When I've dropped
this feathered ball of suffering
I'll spread my wings and hover,
a deathless hawk in the rain
over the green hills of Tir na n-Oc.'

That lame little yellow bird
sings.

Diplomacy

There's rust in the breeze
shaking the lock of the leaves
rifling the petals of the flowers.

It is the sound of the sea
surging through the shore rocks
of Time undermining us.

All so gently, peacefully moving,
the embassies of the ultimate forgetting.

Snail's Pace

A thoughtless boot
will finish it.
For now it makes
its leisurely way across
the rain-drenched
plain of stone
where purple flowers
beckon on the horizon.
It bends its course
toward them
silent as invisibility.
And incrementally
the world advances.

Burning Peat Briquettes

From an anonymous stack in the cold
they're brought
to be individually consumed in the fire.

Though each the same the fire takes from them
a different shape,
and the dance of flame
is nowhere the same for a second.

Too quickly their bevelled rigidity
shrinks to one glowing mass
through the contours of which
pale tongues of flame lick

sealing out the cold,
and the watcher in the cold.

Ship at Dusk

Lit like a birthday cake
it glides from the dying Sun
to the darkening east.

Chock full of idiots
with their idiot distractions
idiot talk,
but how majestic

this icing of stars, these
leisuredly fleeing Pleiades,
this undimmable proof
of beauty's fidelity to distance,

it takes the breath away.

Wexford Harbour

The boats along the quay
are boats
at the bottom of the sea.
Rigged reliquaries
in the warm plankton
of the darkness.

The hold of this night
preserves everything.
Ghosts of memory
are living material
along the boardwalk,
down the sidestreets,
weighing the air
with salt-sweet promise.

Life stops passing by,
but I keep moving.
Though stars are buoys
marking no constellations,
but drift low, close burning,
spilling votive fire
where deeps of feeling are.